hE

This DangerSpot book belongs to:

- -

Published in 2006 by DangerSpot Books Ltd.
Old Bank House,
High Street,
Laxfield,
Woodbridge,
Suffolk.
IP13 8DX.
UK.
www.dangerspot.co.uk

Printed by Proost NV, Turnhout, Belgium.

ISBN 0-9546565-7-1
EAN 9780954656577

The Dangerously Big Bunny

Hedley Griffin

DangerSpot Books Ltd.

'Come and watch the telly!' suggested Harey, lying on the sofa eating a packet of crisps.

'Harey! You're always watching the television and stuffing yourself with the wrong foods. You're putting on weight,' said Scampi. 'You'll become really unhealthy if you carry on like that!'

'You'll become really unhealthy!' repeated Pillow the parrot.

'Would you like a bar of chocolate toffee?' asked Harey.

'Let's go out and play with our skateboards,' suggested Chips, running out of the room.

'Great idea!' said Harey, as he got up in a hurry to rush through the door like
a hare-brained rabbit, as usual, but he suddenly got stuck.'

'That doorway must have shrunk! I can't get through!' said Harey.
'No, it's you! You've got fatter! You've put on so much weight you can't get through the door any more,' said Scampi.

Scampi and Pillow pushed and heaved and heaved and pushed from behind.

Chips pulled his arm while Harey held onto the doorframe.

Suddenly, the door slammed on Harey's fingers.

'Arghh!' he screamed.

The shock of the pain made him leap forward, free of the doorway.

'I won't put my fingers there again,' said Harey, rubbing away the pain.

Outside, Scampi and Chips leapt onto their skateboards.

Harey jumped onto his as well, but it would not move. He was too heavy.

'Oh, dear!' he said.

'Never mind,' said Scampi. 'Let's go to the park and play.'

In the park, Harey sat on one end of the see-saw and Pillow, Scampi and Chips sat on the other end, but it would not move. Harey was too heavy. Even when Pillow jumped up and down on Chips's shoulder it still would not move.

'There must be something wrong with the see-saw,' said Harey.

'It is not balanced properly.'

'It's you that's out of balance,' said Scampi.

'You are too overweight and too heavy.'

'Let's go and play on the swings,' suggested Harey, as he jumped off the see-saw. Immediately, Scampi and Chips and Pillow crashed to the ground on the other end.

'Ow! Ouch!' they all cried.

'That wasn't very good! You should have got off slowly and allowed us to get off as well,' cried Scampi, rubbing her bruised bottom.

Harey tried to sit on the swing but he was too big. He fell off and landed on the ground just as the seat swung back and hit him on the back of his head. 'Oww!' he yelled.

'You must really lose some weight,' advised Scampi, as they all struggled to help him up.

'Shall we go down to the boating-pond?' suggested Chips.

'Yeah! We could buy an ice cream!' said Harey.

'Yeah!' said everyone together.

'Chips had vanilla ice cream, Scampi had strawberry, Pillow had passionfruit and ginger surprise, and Harey had vanilla, strawberry, chocolate, fudge, honey-almond, raspberry ripple, tooti-fruitie, lemon sorbet.

'You'll put on more weight!' said Scampi.

'Would you like a fizzy drink?' asked Harey, offering Scampi a bottle of pop.

'No thanks, I would rather drink water. It's better for you.'

'Let's hire a boat and go rowing on the pond,' suggested Chips.

When Harey managed to join them in the boat he sank it. He was too heavy.

'You really must lose some weight!' said Scampi.

'It's time to go back home for tea,' said Harey,
as they slowly walked out of the park with wet feet.
They had to keep stopping on the way to allow Harey to catch up with them,
because he was too slow.

'I'm exhausted!' said Harey, when they arrived home.

'That's because you are overweight and unhealthy!' said Scampi.

'You really must lose some weight!' said Pillow the parrot.

Harey was so sad to be big and unhealthy he went to the doctor.

The doctor said that being too fat was making him ill.

He told Harey how much better he would feel if he

lost some weight and offered some help and advice.

He had to cut down eating burgers and chips, biscuits, cakes, ice creams, chocolates and sweets.
He soon found he liked eating more fruit and vegetables instead.

He also had to watch less television and do more exercise.

He started walking more and using his bike. He even joined a gym.

He lost weight and became really fit and healthy again. He felt great.

'Who's a pretty boy, then?' said Pillow the parrot.

Place the DangerSpot stickers around your home as a reminder of the dangers and keep your children safe!

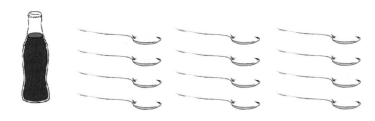

Up to as much as 12 teaspoons of sugar may be present in a 12 oz. fizzy drink.

Approximately 90% of a hotdog is fat.

The recommended maximum amount of daily salt intake for an adult is 6 grams. The daily amount for a child it is a lot less depending on age. A packet of crisps may contain as much as 3 grams, for many children more than the daily maximum recommendation.

• How much do you have to do to work off an average (50g) chocolate bar?
Watching a DVD for 2hrs 45mins or running around for 32mins.
Playing a play station game for 1hr 45mins or going swimming for 20mins.

• People often mistake thirst for hunger. What you might need is a drink of water.

• It's good to share.

• If you want to be strong and healthy, eat 5 portions of fruit and veg a day.

There is a major concern about the increasing numbers of children becoming overweight and obese. Some of the health risks for our future generations include type 2 diabetes, heart disease, certain cancers, stroke, back and joint pain, osteoarthritis, high blood pressure, gallstones, fatty liver, infertility, breathlessness and depression.

Information supplied by TOAST, The Obesity Awareness & Solutions Trust.